*For Sally and Lisa*
**H.M.**

First published 1995
by Walker Books Ltd
87 Vauxhall Walk
London SE11 5HJ

2 4 6 8 10 9 7 5 3 1

Text © 1995 Heather Maisner
Illustrations © 1995 Alan Baron

The right of Heather Maisner to be identified as author of
this work has been asserted by her in accordance
with the Copyright, Designs and Patents Act 1988.

This book has been typeset in Stone Informal and Birch.

Printed in Italy

British Library Cataloguing in Publication Data
A catalogue record for this book is available from the British Library.

ISBN 0-7445-2389-3

# THE MAGIC GLOBE

## A ROUND-THE-WORLD ADVENTURE GAME

HEATHER MAISNER    illustrated by ALAN BARON

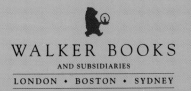

WALKER BOOKS
AND SUBSIDIARIES
LONDON · BOSTON · SYDNEY

CANADA AND ALASKA
Pages 24 & 25

green

UNITED STATES
OF AMERICA
Pages 14 & 15

green and blue

SOUTH AMERICA
Pages 20 & 21

red

yellow

Great Uncle Atlas, a famous travel writer, has sent you a **yellow MAGIC GLOBE** and some instructions.

The globe was given to him by a traveller in the Andes Mountains. When you touch it and say the magic word, it sets off on a journey round the world, changes colour and hides. You too are sent on a journey.

Your task is to search for the globe and follow it back to **THIS PAGE**. But, before you start, read these instructions **VERY CAREFULLY** or you could be left in a faraway place.

## INSTRUCTIONS

1. Touch the yellow globe and say "Zoomafar". When you turn the page, your journey will begin with a choice of two **AMAZING ADVENTURES.**

2. Choose either Amazing Adventure 1 or Amazing Adventure 2. The city where you start has an **orange** sign. Follow **THE ROUTE** to find the globe, which has changed colour and is hiding close to the final clue.

Here are two examples:

3. Find the globe, memorize its colour and turn to the **WORLD MAP** above. Match the colour to a globe on the map. This tells you which place to go to next.

4. Turn to this place, choose an Amazing Adventure and follow **THE ROUTE**. Each time you find the globe, return to the map. If you are sent to the same place more than once, choose the other route.

5. Keep going until the globe becomes **yellow** again and leads you back to **THIS PAGE**.

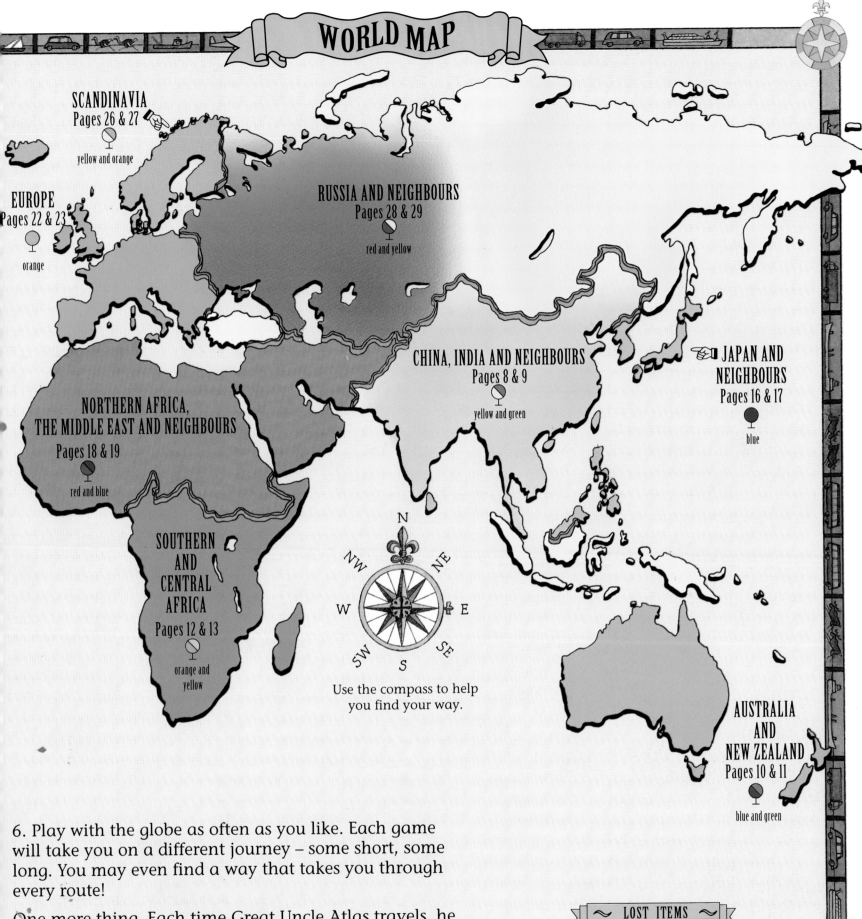

# WORLD MAP

**SCANDINAVIA**
Pages 26 & 27
yellow and orange

**EUROPE**
Pages 22 & 23
orange

**RUSSIA AND NEIGHBOURS**
Pages 28 & 29
red and yellow

**JAPAN AND NEIGHBOURS**
Pages 16 & 17
blue

**NORTHERN AFRICA,
THE MIDDLE EAST AND NEIGHBOURS**
Pages 18 & 19
red and blue

**CHINA, INDIA AND NEIGHBOURS**
Pages 8 & 9
yellow and green

**SOUTHERN
AND
CENTRAL
AFRICA**
Pages 12 & 13
orange and yellow

Use the compass to help
you find your way.

**AUSTRALIA
AND
NEW ZEALAND**
Pages 10 & 11
blue and green

6. Play with the globe as often as you like. Each game
will take you on a different journey – some short, some
long. You may even find a way that takes you through
every route!

One more thing. Each time Great Uncle Atlas travels, he
loses some of his belongings. Please look out for them
and bring them back with you. There are 22 items.

Have fun. Don't get lost. And look out for Great Uncle Atlas
too! You'll find him four times.

~ LOST ITEMS ~

torch, paintbrush, magnifying glass, calculator,
key, yellow pencil, watch, scissors, paperclip,
rucksack, spectacles, ruler, green pencil, notepad,
umbrella, sticky tape, bottle of ink, camera,
fountain pen, penknife, envelope, pencil sharpener

**You have arrived in** MADRAS **on the east coast of India. This vast land has many different languages and religions.**

### ~ THE ROUTE ~

☞ Go by rail NE to the crowded city of **CALCUTTA**.

☞ Follow the road NE over the sacred **RIVER GANGES** to **DHAKA**, capital of Bangladesh. Continue N to **MOUNT EVEREST**, the highest mountain in the world at 8,848 m. The *yeti* – abominable snowman – is said to live here.

☞ Follow the road E to **LHASA**, capital of Tibet. Then go by road N through the mountains and E all the way to **LANZHOU** on the **YELLOW RIVER** in China. This is often called the world's muddiest river.

☞ Go NW by train beside the Great Wall and on to the oasis town of **TURPAN**. The Great Wall was begun 2,000 years ago to protect China from invaders from the north. It stretches over 5,660 km.

☞ Go W, around the **TAKLAMAKAN DESERT,** to **KASHGAR**. Do not wander into the desert. Its name means: "If you go in, you'll never come out".

☞ Journey S through the spectacular mountains that separate China from Pakistan, to **ISLAMABAD**, capital of Pakistan.

☞ Continue S by road to **LAHORE**. Then take the train SE over the border to **NEW DELHI**, capital of India. Indian trains are very crowded; you may have to ride on the roof!

☞ SEEK THE MAGIC GLOBE
Now it is orange and yellow.

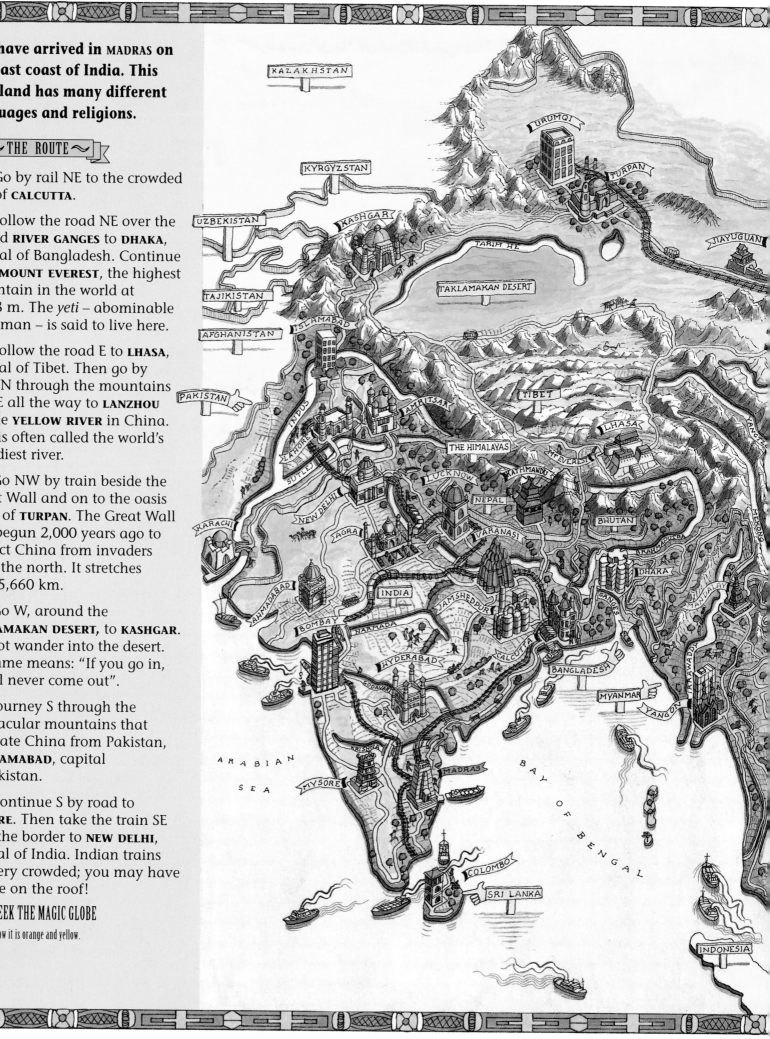

**You have arrived in HARBIN in north-east China. More people live here than in any other country. Over one billion people in the world are Chinese.**

### ~ THE ROUTE ~

☞ Go SW by car past **SHENYANG** to **BEIJING**, China's capital. Visit the Forbidden City where the Imperial family lived. For 500 years no ordinary person could enter here.

☞ Take the train S to **JINAN**. Then follow the **YELLOW RIVER** SW to **ZHENGZHOU** and go on to **XI'AN**, once the capital of China. Visit lifesize models of 8,000 soldiers buried over 2,000 years ago.

☞ Go by road SW past **CHENGDU**, through the region where giant pandas live, to **LESHAN**. Can you see that huge figure? It's the largest statue of Buddha in the world – 71 m high.

☞ Continue along the road S past **KUNMING** to **HANOI**, capital of Vietnam. Then go to **BANGKOK**, to the SW. You are now in the capital of Thailand.

☞ Sail S by ship to **SINGAPORE**, a small island but a major port, where it is hot and humid all year round.

☞ Sail NE across the **SOUTH CHINA SEA** all the way to **MANILA**. You are in the capital of the Philippines, which includes over 7,000 islands.

☞ Now go by ship NW to **HONG KONG**. Its name means "fragrant harbour" and it is one of the most densely populated places on earth.

☞ **SEEK THE MAGIC GLOBE**
Now it is blue and green.

**You have arrived in** ALBANY **in the south-west of Australia, a country with desert in the centre and tropical rainforest in the north. This country is sometimes called Oz.**

### ~ THE ROUTE ~

☞ Go by coach N to **PERTH**, where the sun shines an average eight hours every day. Go swimming and sailing in the ocean.

☞ Fly E to the gold-mining town of **KALGOORLIE**. Take a lift cage down under the ground to explore a gold mine.

☞ Travel by road all the way to **ADELAIDE**, to the SE. Visit the nearby Investigator Science Museum – hands-on fun for everyone. Then have a "barbie" – barbecue – on the beach.

☞ Take the train NW to **ALICE SPRINGS,** where the land is completely parched. Explore the desert landscape by camel.

☞ Journey SW to **AYERS ROCK**, the world's largest monolith (single block of stone). This is a sacred place to Aboriginal people, Australia's earliest inhabitants, who call it Uluru.

☞ Return to **ALICE SPRINGS**, then ride N in a jeep past **TENNANT CREEK** to **DARWIN**. Hot and sticky? Take a boat ride through the vast wetlands but look out for crocodiles! See ancient Aboriginal rock art.

☞ Go by bus to the old pearling port of **BROOME**, to the SW. Visit nearby dinosaur footprints, said to be 130 million years old.

☞ **SEEK THE MAGIC GLOBE**
Now it is orange and yellow.

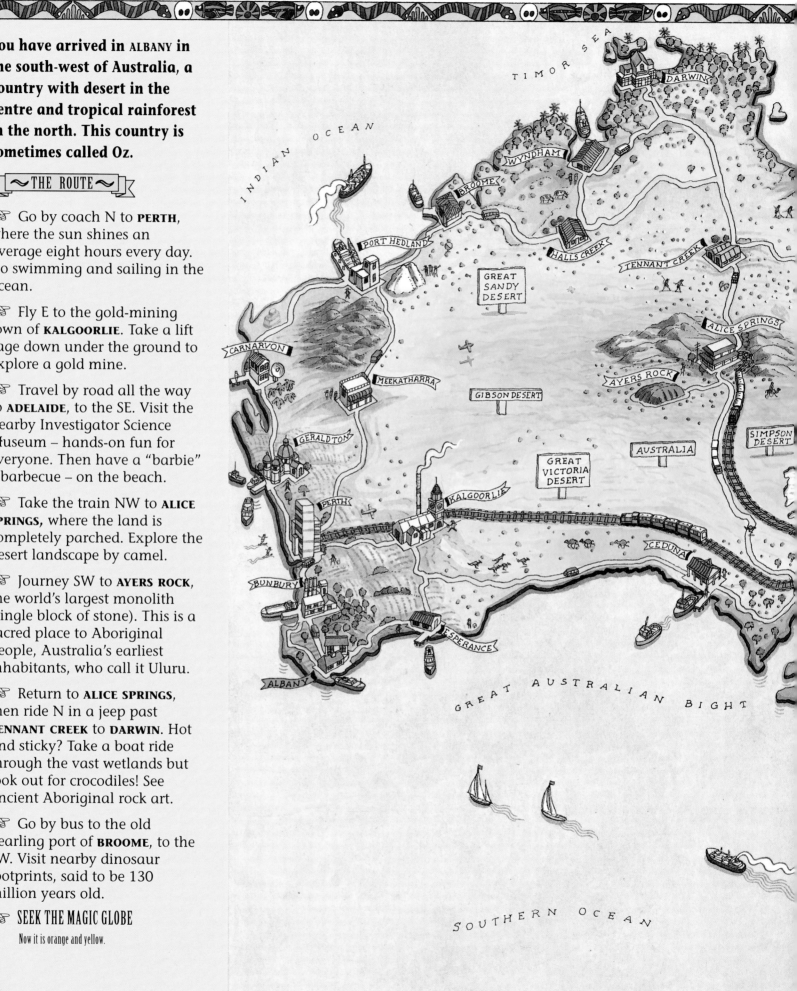

**You have arrived in BLUFF at the south end of New Zealand. The Maoris – the first people to live here – called this mountainous country the "land of the long white cloud".**

## ~ THE ROUTE ~

☞ Follow the road NE past **DUNEDIN** to **CHRISTCHURCH**. Pass sheep stations on the way. New Zealand has more sheep than people. There are at least 20 sheep to each person.

☞ Take the boat NE to **WELLINGTON**, capital of New Zealand. Hold on to your hat! In this city, known as "Windy Wellington", winds can blow up to 100 km an hour.

☞ Go by car N to **ROTORUA**. Tired? Visit hot springs and have a mud bath; see geysers over 30 m high. Then go N to **AUCKLAND**, the largest city in New Zealand.

☞ Cruise NW by boat across the sea to **SYDNEY** in Australia. Do you see that building in the shape of sails? It's the famous Sydney Opera House.

☞ Travel by train N past **PORT MACQUARIE** and **COFFS HARBOUR** to **BRISBANE**. Visit the nearby Koala Sanctuary and see animals found only in Australia.

☞ Go W by car past **TOOWOOMBA** to **CHARLEVILLE** and NW to **WINTON**. Do you see that large statue? It's Banjo Paterson, the poet and song-writer, who wrote "Waltzing Matilda".

☞ Now go N to **CAIRNS** where it's hot all year round. Visit the Great Barrier Reef and see exotic underwater creatures in the largest coral reef in the world.

☞ **SEEK THE MAGIC GLOBE**
Now it is green and blue.

You have arrived in MOGADISHU, capital of Somalia on the north-east coast of Africa. Africa is where people say mankind began.

## ~ THE ROUTE ~

☞ Sail SW along the coast to MOMBASA. Then go NW by train to NAIROBI. This is the capital of Kenya.

☞ Follow the road S to MT KILIMANJARO and climb to the top of the snow-capped summit. You are now at the highest point in Africa.

☞ Take a hot-air balloon NW past herds of wildebeest and zebra to LAKE VICTORIA. Fly on to KAMPALA, capital of Uganda.

☞ Go by road across the border to KISANGANI, to the W. You are now in Zaire. Visit pygmies in the nearby rainforest. They are under 1.5 m tall.

☞ Feeling hot? Take a river boat along the RIVER ZAIRE to LISALA, to the NW. This river used to be called the Congo.

☞ Go by road NW across the OUBANGUI RIVER to BANGUI, capital of the Central African Republic.

☞ Continue NW by bus to BOUAR. Do you see those huge standing stones? They were put up by an ancient civilization thousands of years ago.

☞ Go SW by bus past YAOUNDÉ to LAMBARÉNÉ in Gabon. Want to see some elephants? Few people live here so the forests are full of wildlife.

☞ Continue SE by car to BRAZZAVILLE, capital of the Congo.

☞ SEEK THE MAGIC GLOBE
Now it is blue.

# You have arrived in SWAKOPMUND on the south-west coast of Africa in Namibia. This country is mostly desert with some of the world's highest sand-dunes – up to 304 m high.

## ~ THE ROUTE ~

☞ Take the train E to **WINDHOEK**. Then follow the road E through the **KALAHARI DESERT** to **MAUN** in Botswana. Pass Bushmen on the way. They are among the earliest-known inhabitants of southern Africa.

☞ Continue E over the border to the ruins of **GREAT ZIMBABWE**. This was a huge city about 600 years ago.

☞ Go by road past **BULAWAYO** to **VICTORIA FALLS**, to the NW. This waterfall is known locally as "the smoke that thunders". Did you bring an umbrella? Spray can fly up to 500 m.

☞ Continue by road NE past zebras and elephants to **LILONGWE**, capital of Malawi. Hungry? Have a feast of bananas, guavas and mangoes.

☞ Go E to the port of **PEMBA**. Stow away on a boat sailing SE to **MAHAJANGA** on the island of Madagascar. Beware sharks on the way!

☞ Go S by car to **TOLIARA**. Visit a petrified forest and see fossilized trees. Then fly SW to **MAPUTO**, capital of Mozambique.

☞ Take the train into South Africa past **JOHANNESBURG** to **KIMBERLEY**, to the SW. See that big hole? It's the world's biggest man-made hole and was dug for diamonds.

☞ **SEEK THE MAGIC GLOBE**
Now it is green and blue.

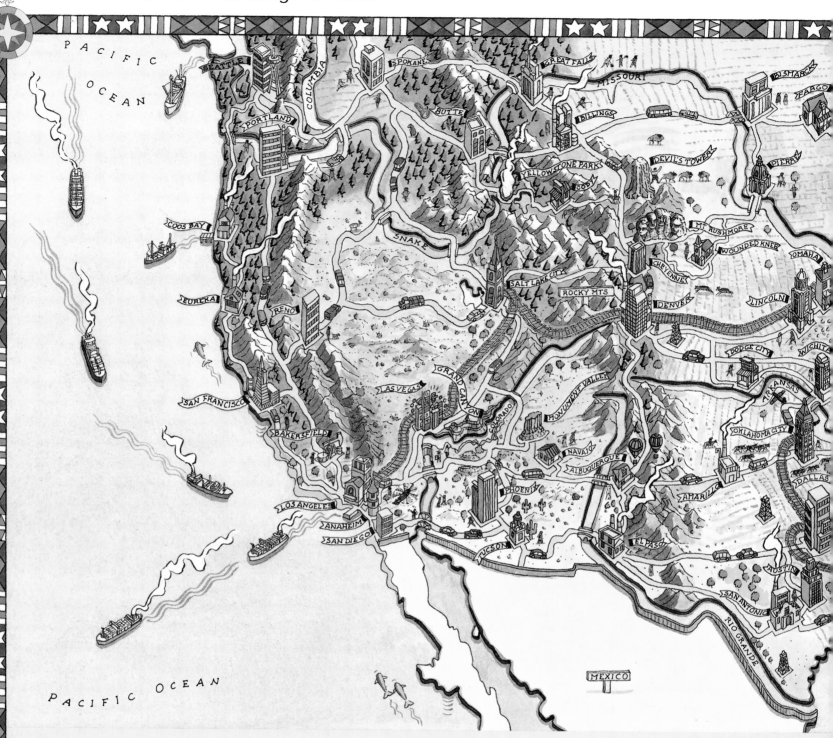

**You have arrived in SEATTLE on the north-west coast of the United States of America. This huge country stretches from the Pacific Ocean in the west to the Atlantic Ocean in the east. It also includes Alaska and Hawaii.**

## ~ THE ROUTE ~

☞ Sail S through the Pacific Ocean to **SAN FRANCISCO**. This city built on 40 hills grew as a result of the gold rush in 1849.

☞ Go by car SE to **LOS ANGELES**. See Hollywood, home of the movies, then go on to nearby **ANAHEIM** and visit Disneyland.

☞ Fly NE by helicopter to the **GRAND CANYON**. Look down steep cliffs to the Colorado River snaking through the valley 1.6 km below.

☞ Cycle S past **PHOENIX**, then along the Apache Trail – the old Apache tribe's route across the land – to **TUCSON**. See nearby giant cacti that can grow to 13 m and live up to 200 years.

☞ Go by car E past **EL PASO** and **SAN ANTONIO** to **HOUSTON**. Visit the LBJ Space Center and see the Mission Control that landed the first man on the moon in 1969.

☞ Take the train NW to **OKLAHOMA CITY**. Pass large herds of cattle on the way. Go NW by plane to **DENVER**.

☞ Continue N to **MOUNT RUSHMORE**. Do you see those huge faces carved into the cliffs? They are portraits of four US presidents.

☞ **SEEK THE MAGIC GLOBE**

Now it is blue.

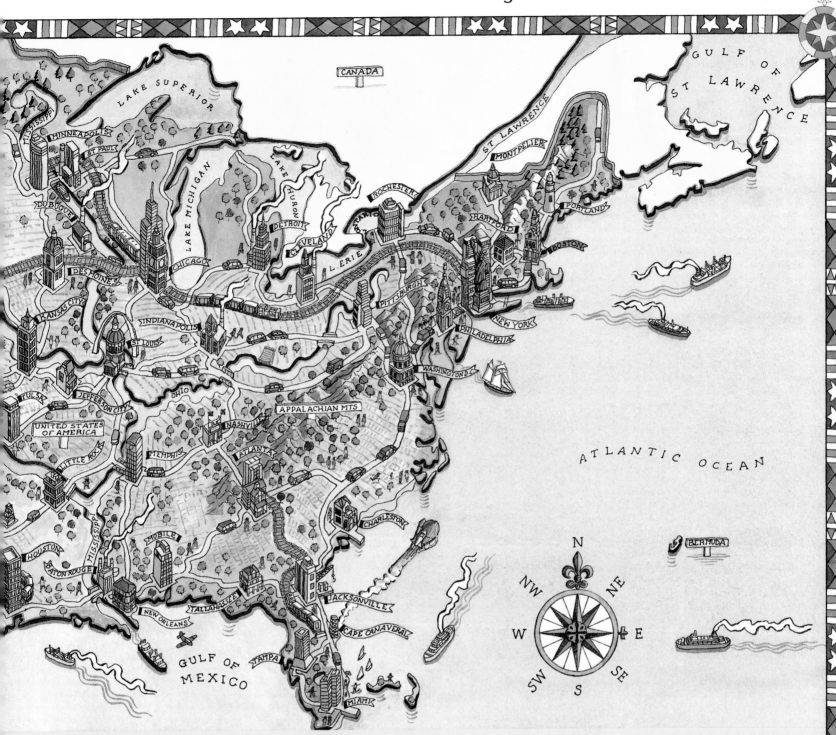

**You have arrived in BOSTON on the north-east coast of the United States of America, a country made up of 50 separate states. It was here that the War of Independence began in 1775.**

~ THE ROUTE ~

☞ Take the Greyhound Bus SW to **NEW YORK** and visit the Statue of Liberty. Then go SW to **WASHINGTON D.C.**, capital of the United States and home of the US government.

☞ Go by car NW to **DETROIT**, known as Motor City. Visit the Henry Ford Museum. See early cars and the bicycle shop where the Wright brothers built the first plane.

☞ Continue W to **CHICAGO**. Take the lift to the top of the Sears Tower and discover how the world looks from its tallest building.

☞ Catch a train NW to **MINNEAPOLIS** – its name means "city of water" – and you are now by the mighty **MISSISSIPPI RIVER**. Go by boat S to **SAINT LOUIS**.

☞ Continue S by boat, past **MEMPHIS**, all the way to **NEW ORLEANS**, where jazz music began.

☞ Now fly SE across the **GULF OF MEXICO** to **MIAMI**. Then go N to **CAPE CANAVERAL**. Just look at that rocket! This is the Kennedy Space Center, where manned space flights are launched.

☞ Take a train NW to **ATLANTA**. Thirsty? Have a Coca-Cola. It was invented right here!

☞ **SEEK THE MAGIC GLOBE**

Now it is red.

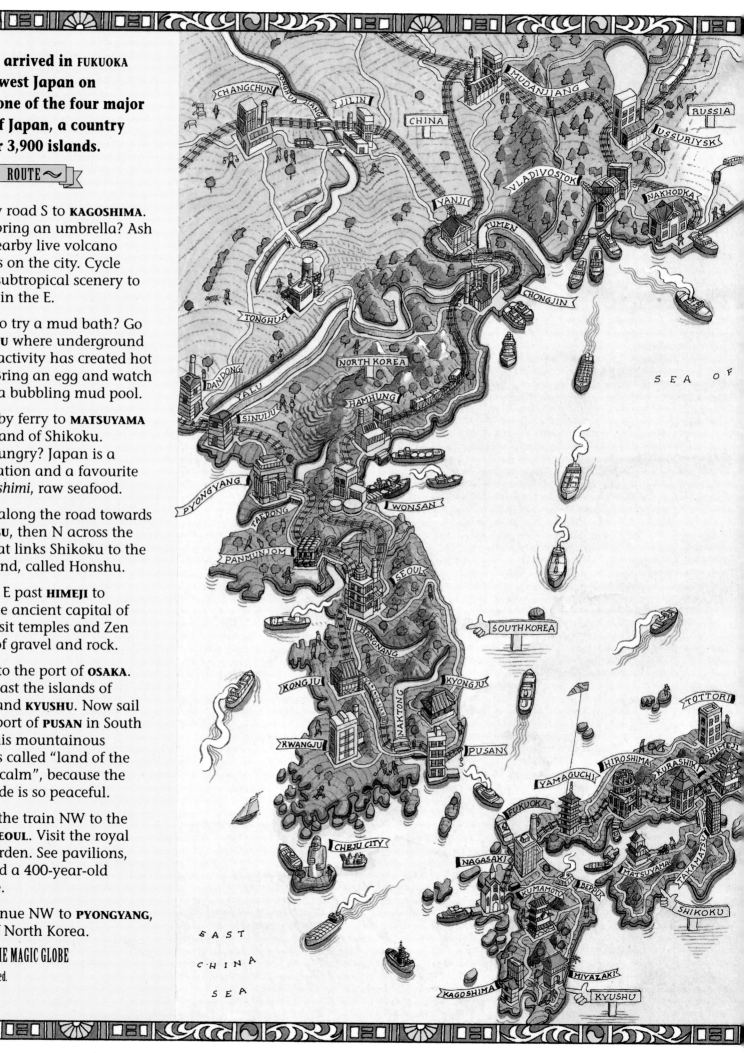

**You have arrived in** FUKUOKA **in south-west Japan on Kyushu, one of the four major islands of Japan, a country with over 3,900 islands.**

## ~ THE ROUTE ~

☞ Go by road S to **KAGOSHIMA**. Did you bring an umbrella? Ash from a nearby live volcano often falls on the city. Cycle through subtropical scenery to **MIYAZAKI** in the E.

☞ Like to try a mud bath? Go N to **BEPPU** where underground volcanic activity has created hot springs. Bring an egg and watch it boil in a bubbling mud pool.

☞ Go E by ferry to **MATSUYAMA** on the island of Shikoku. Feeling hungry? Japan is a fishing nation and a favourite dish is *sashimi*, raw seafood.

☞ Go E along the road towards **TAKAMATSU**, then N across the bridge that links Shikoku to the main island, called Honshu.

☞ Cycle E past **HIMEJI** to **KYOTO**, the ancient capital of Japan. Visit temples and Zen gardens of gravel and rock.

☞ Go S to the port of **OSAKA**. Sail SW past the islands of **SHIKOKU** and **KYUSHU**. Now sail N to the port of **PUSAN** in South Korea. This mountainous country is called "land of the morning calm", because the countryside is so peaceful.

☞ Take the train NW to the capital, **SEOUL**. Visit the royal Secret Garden. See pavilions, ponds and a 400-year-old plum tree.

☞ Continue NW to **PYONGYANG**, capital of North Korea.

☞ **SEEK THE MAGIC GLOBE**
   Now it is red.

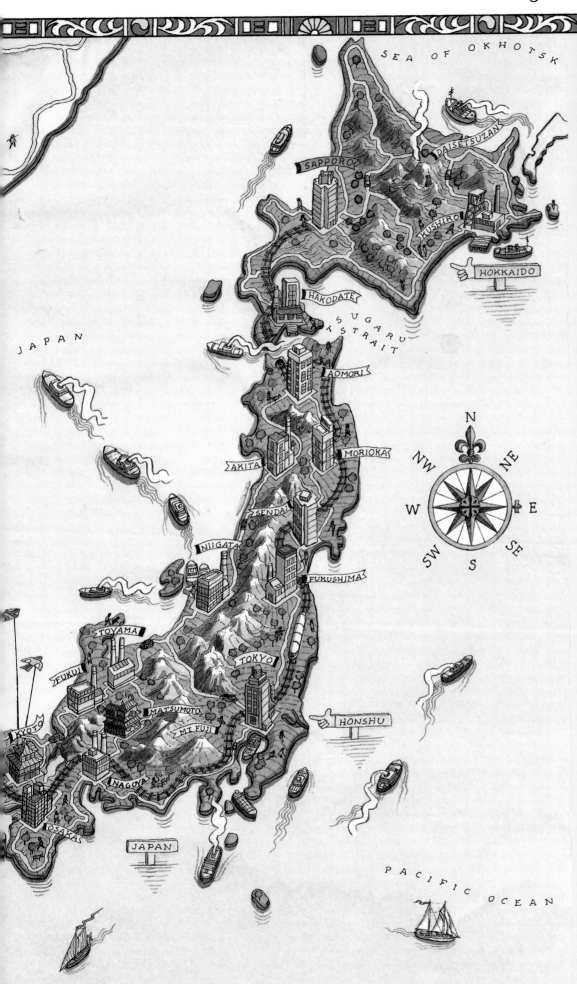

**You have arrived in SAPPORO on Hokkaido, the major island in north Japan. In winter the temperature often falls to −30°C.**

### ～ THE ROUTE ～

☞ Catch a bus NE to **DAISETSUZAN** Nature Park and hike through the mountains. Japan's largest wild animal, the brown bear, lives here.

☞ Go SE to **KUSHIRO** and on to **HAKODATE** in the SW. Take a train under the **TSUGARU STRAIT** to **AOMORI** through the world's longest under-sea tunnel – 54 km.

☞ Continue S to **MORIOKA**. Then travel at 240 km per hour on the Bullet Train to **FUKUSHIMA**. You are in the main rice-growing area and a Japanese word for rice – *gohan* – also means meal.

☞ Continue by train to **TOKYO**, capital of Japan. Visit shops selling the world's latest electronic equipment.

☞ Go by road SW to **MT FUJI**, Japan's highest mountain. This dormant volcano is often called "mountain where the gods dwell".

☞ Continue on to **NAGOYA,** to the W. Like to know how the *samurai* lived? Travel NE to **MATSUMOTO** and explore the six-storey black castle, known as Crow Castle.

☞ Go by car to **NIIGATA**, to the NE. You are now in one of the heaviest snowfall regions in the world, where the winds blow across from Siberia in Russia.

☞ Sail NW by ship across the **SEA OF JAPAN** to **VLADIVOSTOK** in Russia. This is the last stop on the Trans-Siberian railway, which runs all the way from Moscow.

☞ **SEEK THE MAGIC GLOBE**

Now it is green.

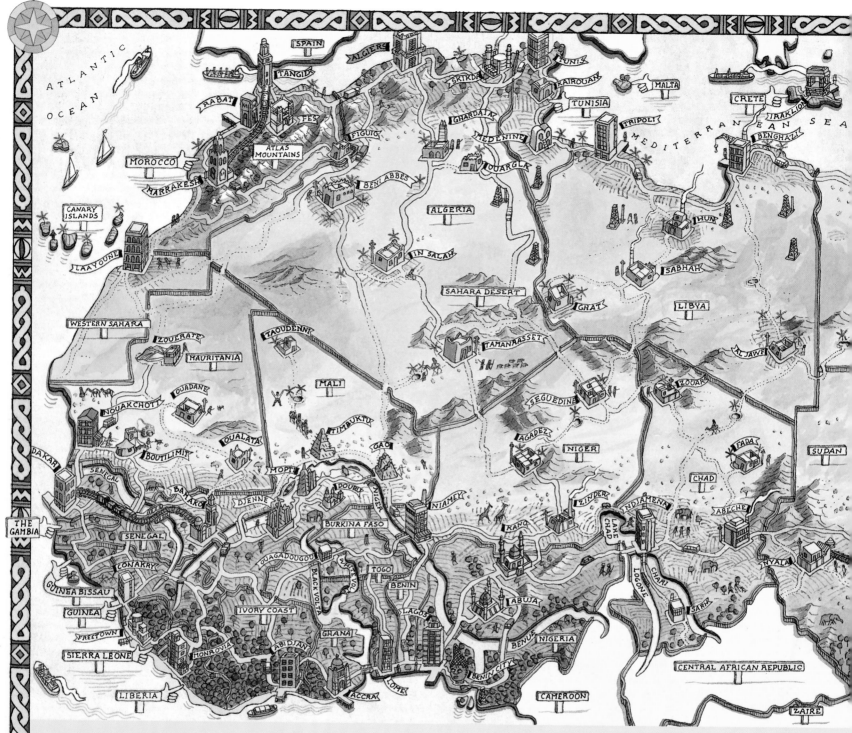

**You have arrived in ALGIERS, capital of Algeria, on the north coast of Africa. Africa includes more than 50 countries.**

### ~ THE ROUTE ~

☞ Go by road W to **TANGIER** in Morocco. Thirsty? Visit the narrow streets of the *medina* – old city – and stop for a glass of mint tea.

☞ Catch a train to **MARRAKESH** in the SW. Explore the winding alleys of the famous *souk* – market.

☞ Make your way E across the snow-capped **ATLAS MOUNTAINS** to **BENI ABBÈS** in Algeria. You are now in the Sahara Desert, the largest desert in the world.

☞ Continue to **TAMANRASSET** in the SE. Can you see blue-robed *Tuaregs* with goats? They are nomads who move from place to place in search of grazing.

☞ Fill your flask with water and ride SW by camel to **TIMBUKTU** in Mali. This was once the centre of the gold trade in West Africa.

☞ Hot and tired? You're in luck. It's the wet season and the **NIGER RIVER** is high. Paddle in a dugout canoe SW past **DJENNÉ** to **BAMAKO**. Avoid the hippos as you go!

☞ Ride SE on a truck through the Ivory Coast to **ABIDJAN**. Go swimming in the ocean.

☞ Now catch a boat going W round the bulge of Africa to **FREETOWN**, capital of Sierra Leone. This means "lion mountains".

☞ **SEEK THE MAGIC GLOBE**

Now it is blue and green.

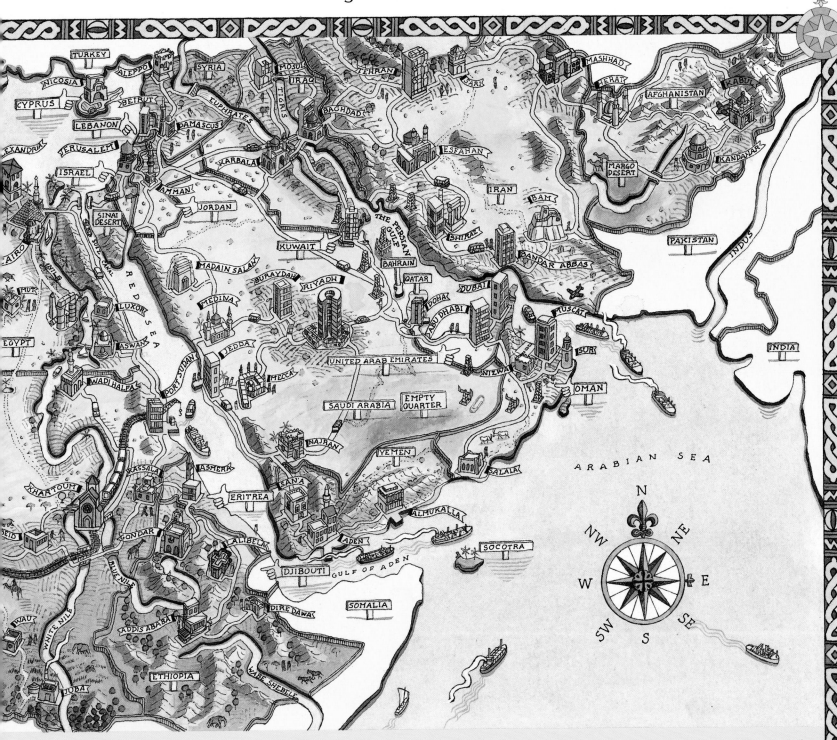

**You have arrived in KABUL, capital of Afghanistan, in the north-east. Afghanistan is a landlocked country with great mountains and burning deserts, valleys and plains.**

## ~ THE ROUTE ~

☞ Fly SW all the way to **MUSCAT**, capital of Oman, in the Middle East. On the way see camels moving across the **MARGO DESERT** – "Desert of Death". Now take a ferry NW to **BANDAR ABBAS** in Iran.

☞ Go by bus to **SHIRAZ**, to the NW. Visit palaces built over 2,500 years ago.

☞ Continue by bus NW past the city of **ESFAHAN** and across the border to **BAGHDAD**, the capital of Iraq. You are now in the region known in ancient times as Mesopotamia.

☞ Go by car SW to **AMMAN**, capital of Jordan. Continue NW to **JERUSALEM**, capital of Israel. Visit holy sites of three religions: Judaism, Islam and Christianity.

☞ Take a bus SW across the **SINAI DESERT** to the **SUEZ CANAL**. This shipping canal links the Mediterranean Sea, in the N, with the Red Sea.

☞ Continue W to **CAIRO**, capital of Egypt. Sail along the **RIVER NILE**, the longest river in the world, to **LUXOR**, to the SE. Many pharaohs were buried near by in the Valley of the Kings.

☞ Follow the river S past **WADI HALFA** to **KHARTOUM**, capital of Sudan.

☞ SEEK THE MAGIC GLOBE

Now it is yellow.

**You have arrived in** RIO DE JANEIRO, **halfway down the east coast of Brazil. This is the largest country in South America and the only one where Portuguese is the national language. Most speak Spanish.**

~ THE ROUTE ~

☞ Go N by bus to **SALVADOR.** See boys practising *capoeira* – a form of martial arts and dance, performed to the rhythm of local music. Continue NE to **RECIFE.**

☞ Go by bus to **BELÉM,** to the NW. Then sail W along the **AMAZON RIVER** to **MANAUS.** Listen to the hoots, chirrups, clicks and hisses of the wildlife. You are travelling through the world's largest rainforest.

☞ Fly NW past the **ANGEL FALLS** to **CARACAS,** capital of Venezuela. This waterfall, the highest in the world, plunges 979 m from a flat-topped mountain.

☞ Go SW by bus past **BOGOTÁ,** capital of Colombia, and on to **QUITO,** capital of Ecuador. Visit ancient stone statues at **SAN AGUSTÍN.**

☞ Go S to **GUAYAQUIL,** then sail W to the **GALÁPAGOS ISLANDS.** Look out for giant tortoises and other creatures unique to these islands.

☞ Fly SE past **LIMA,** capital of Peru, and on to **NAZCA.** See those strange drawings in the desert? They were made 2,000 years ago.

☞ Ride a donkey NE to **CUZCO,** once the capital of the Inca Empire, which stretched from Colombia in the N to Chile in the S. Visit Inca ruins.

☞ **SEEK THE MAGIC GLOBE**

Now it is green.

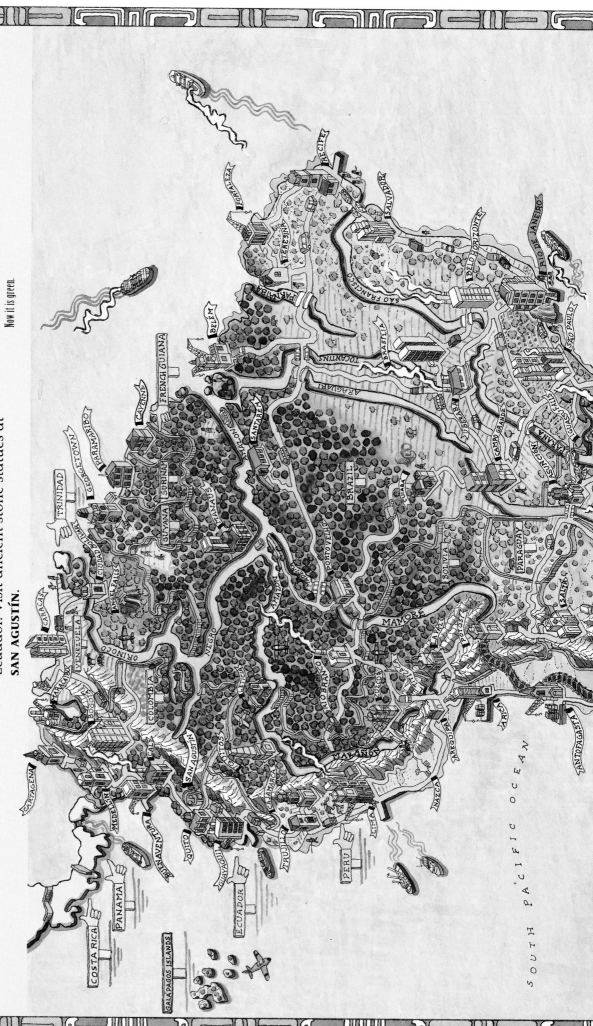

SOUTH ATLANTIC OCEAN

SOUTH GEORGIA

FALKLAND ISLANDS

STANLEY

TIERRA DEL FUEGO

USHUAIA

PUNTA ARENAS

PUERTO MONTT

CHILE

CONCEPCIÓN

SANTIAGO

ATACAMA DESERT

SAN JUAN

CÓRDOBA

ROSARIO

TUCUMÁN

PARAGUAY

BAHÍA BLANCA

ARGENTINA

COLORADO

BARILOCHE

ANDES MOUNTAINS

COMODORO RIVADAVIA

RÍO GALLEGOS

TRELEW

MAR DEL PLATA

BUENOS AIRES

MONTEVIDEO

URUGUAY

PORTO ALEGRE

**You have arrived in USHUAIA at the southern tip of Argentina. Here on the island of Tierra del Fuego – "Land of Fire" – you are as far south as you can go before Antarctica.**

☛ ~ THE ROUTE ~

☛ Fly N to **TRELEW**. You are crossing the flat region known as Patagonia, which comes from a Spanish word for big feet.

☛ Journey by bus NW to **BARILOCHE**. Go skiing or hiking in the Andes Mountains.

☛ Take the train NE across the *pampas* – grassy plains – to **BAHÍA BLANCA** and on to **BUENOS AIRES**, Argentina's capital.

☛ Go by car NE to **PORTO ALEGRE**. See *gauchos* – cowboys – on horseback. They look after large herds of cattle.

☛ Fly NW to **ASUNCIÓN**, capital of Paraguay. Ride on a truck NW over scrubland to **POTOSÍ** in Bolivia, one of the highest cities in the world at 4,200 m.

☛ Go by train SW to **ANTOFAGASTA**. You are crossing the **ATACAMA DESERT**, the driest desert in the world. Parts of this desert have never seen rain nor many living plants or animals.

☛ Continue S by train to **SANTIAGO**, capital of Chile. This long, thin country lies between the Pacific Ocean and the Andes Mountains, which stretch the whole length of South America.

☛ **SEEK THE MAGIC GLOBE**
Now it is yellow and orange.

You have arrived in LISBON, capital of Portugal in southwest Europe. Europe, which includes parts of Russia, has over 30 countries.

### ～ THE ROUTE ～

☞ Go by car NE to **MADRID**, capital of Spain. Then go E past **ZARAGOZA** to **BARCELONA** on the Mediterranean Sea. Hungry? Try *paella*, a rice dish with meat and seafood.

☞ Go by bus NE past the **PYRENEES**, the mountains that separate Spain from France, to **NÎMES**. Continue SE to the port of **MARSEILLE**.

☞ Go N by road past **LYON**, once the capital of Gaul – ancient France – to **STRASBOURG**, home of the European parliament.

☞ Sail along the **RIVER RHINE** past **BONN** to **COLOGNE** in the N. Go carefully! A maiden called the Lorelei is said to sit on a rock and lure sailors to their death with her singing.

☞ Cycle NW to **AMSTERDAM**, capital of the Netherlands. Then go by bus SW past **BRUSSELS**, capital of Belgium, to **PARIS**, capital of France. Climb the Eiffel Tower.

☞ Fly NW all the way to **DUBLIN**, capital of the Republic of Ireland. This city was founded by the Vikings.

☞ Take the ferry E to **HOLYHEAD** in Wales. Then go by bus SE to **LONDON**, capital of the United Kingdom. Do you see that clock tower? It's called Big Ben.

☞ Now go by train NW to **EDINBURGH**, capital of Scotland. Visit the castle. Then go to the Museum of Childhood.

☞ **SEEK THE MAGIC GLOBE**

Now it is red and blue.

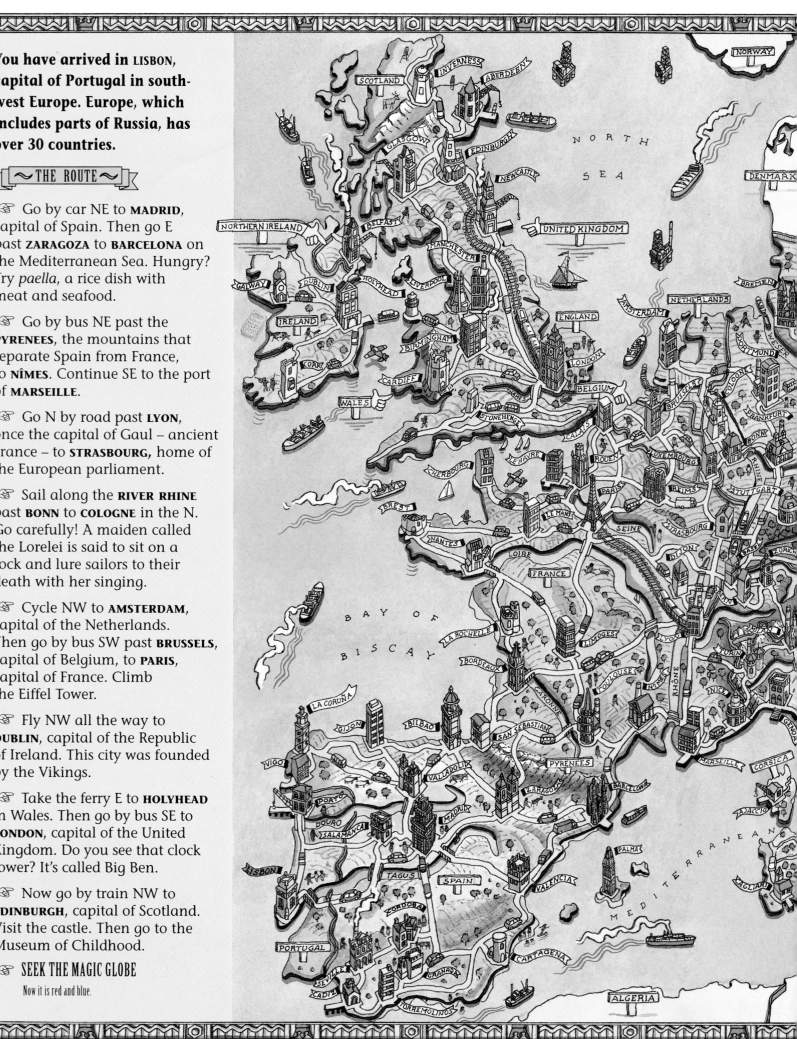

**You have arrived in** ROME, **capital of Italy, the country in the shape of a boot in the Mediterranean Sea.**

☞ **◁~ THE ROUTE ~▷**

☞  Go NW by bus to **PISA**. Can you see that leaning tower? It's the bell tower of Pisa's cathedral, built in the 12th century.

☞  Continue NE to **VENICE** where there are canals instead of streets. Tour the city by waterbus.

☞  Follow the road N over the Alps, which form Italy's northern border, to **MUNICH** in Germany.

☞  Take the train N to **BERLIN**, capital of Germany. See the remains of the Berlin Wall, which divided the city for 30 years until 1990.

☞  Follow the **RIVER ODER** SE to **WROCLAW** in Poland. Then take the road SW to **PRAGUE**. You are now in the capital of the Czech Republic.

☞  Go by car SE to **BUDAPEST**, capital of Hungary, on the **RIVER DANUBE**. Feeling hungry? Try apple strudel – light, thin pastry filled with apples, raisins and nuts.

☞  Sail down the **DANUBE** to **BELGRADE** in the SE. This river flows through eight countries.

☞  Do you dare visit Dracula's castle? Go E to **TIRGOVISTE** where the real Count Dracula lived. Then go on to **BUCHAREST**, capital of Romania.

☞  Now fly SW to **ATHENS**, capital of Greece. Visit the ruins of the Acropolis, built 2,500 years ago.

☞ **SEEK THE MAGIC GLOBE**

Now it is yellow and green.

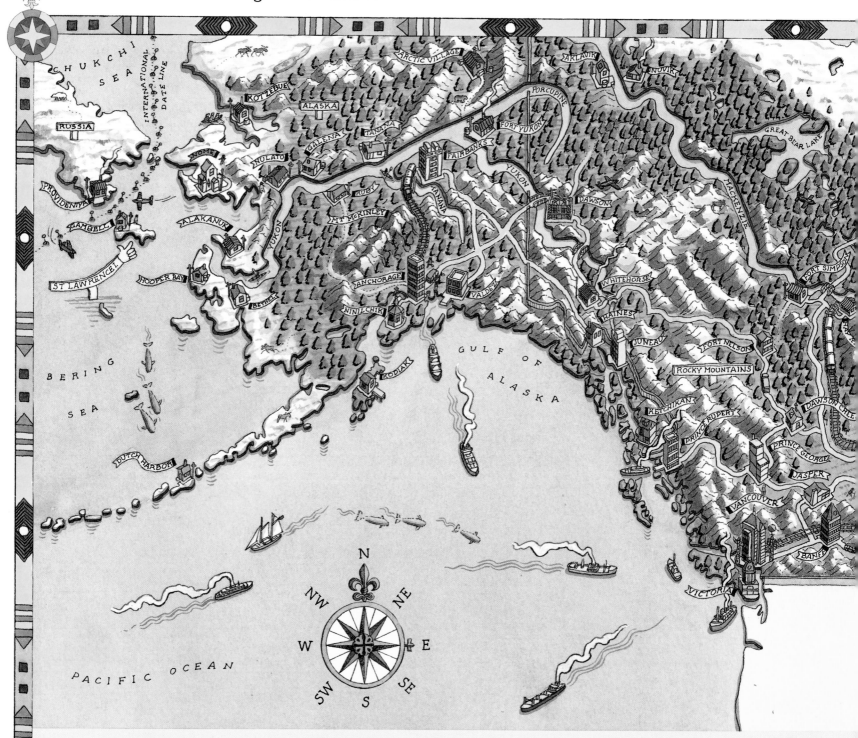

**You have arrived in NOME on the west coast of Alaska. This vast wilderness is the largest state in the United States of America.**

### ~ THE ROUTE ~

☞ It's Sunday. Fly SW past **GAMBELL** on **ST LAWRENCE ISLAND** and across the International Date Line. This imaginary line marks the place where each new day begins. Here it is Monday! Turn back and fly E to **ALAKANUK** where it is still Sunday.

☞ Paddle in a *kayak* – small canoe – up the **YUKON RIVER** to **TANANA** in the NE. Then go SE to **FAIRBANKS**. Take the train S past **MT MCKINLEY**, the highest mountain in North America, to **ANCHORAGE**.

☞ Go by road NE to **DAWSON** in Canada. This was once a booming gold-mining town, the centre of the Klondike gold rush 100 years ago.

☞ Catch a plane and fly E to **YELLOWKNIFE**. Look down on mountains, home to moose and grizzly bears. Go fishing when you arrive.

☞ Sail SW across **GREAT SLAVE LAKE** to **HAY RIVER**. Take the train to **EDMONTON**, to the SE. Then continue S to **CALGARY**. Interested in dinosaurs? Visit the nearby dinosaur park.

☞ Go by bus W past **BANFF** to **VANCOUVER**. Do you see those totem poles? They were made by native tribes such as the Haida, who have lived here for thousands of years.

☞ **SEEK THE MAGIC GLOBE**
Now it is red and yellow.

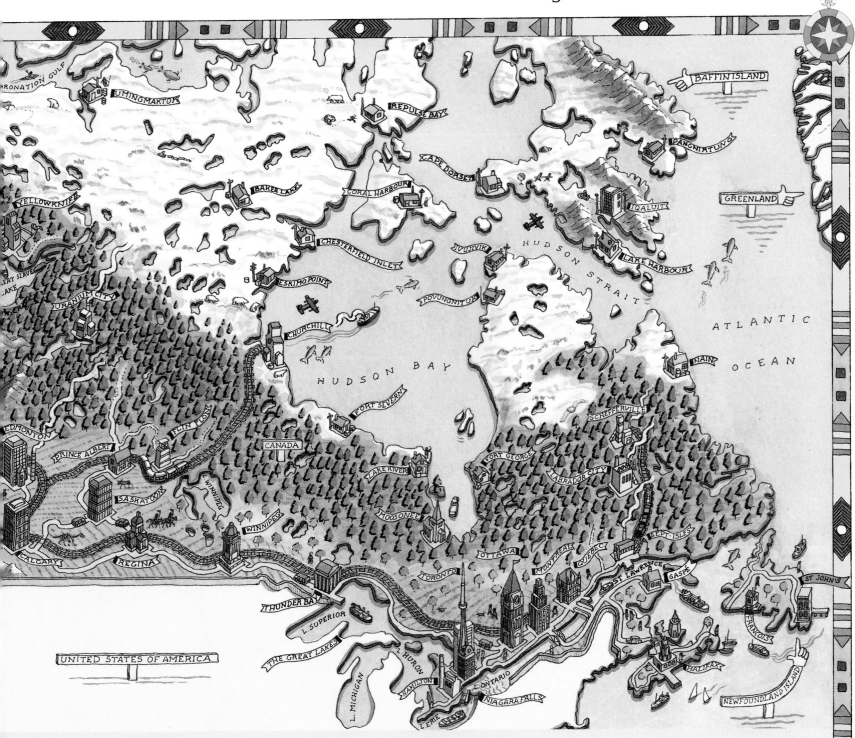

**You have arrived in ST JOHN'S on NEWFOUNDLAND ISLAND in south-east Canada. Many parts of this huge country are uninhabited.**

### ~ THE ROUTE ~

☞ Take a boat W to **GASPÉ** at the start of the **ST LAWRENCE SEAWAY**, the world's longest canal system.

☞ Go SW by boat past **MONTREAL** in French-speaking Canada as far as **NIAGARA FALLS** in English-speaking Canada.

☞ Sail across the **GREAT LAKES** NW to **THUNDER BAY**. These lakes form part of the border between Canada and the United States.

☞ Take a bus W past **WINNIPEG** to **REGINA**. Do you see those men on horseback? They are known as Mounties – Royal Canadian Mounted Police.

☞ Go by car past **SASKATOON** to **PRINCE ALBERT**, to the N. See moose on the way. You are in "big sky country" now, where wheat grows across vast prairie lands.

☞ Catch the train NE to **CHURCHILL**. Tour the flat, frozen land and see polar bears.

☞ Fly in a skiplane NE over **HUDSON BAY** to **IQALUIT** on **BAFFIN ISLAND**. Look down on beluga whales.

☞ Go NW by snowmobile to **CAPE DORSET**. Visit an Inuit – Eskimo – family. Inuit means "people" in their language.

☞ **SEEK THE MAGIC GLOBE**
Now it is yellow and orange.

**You have arrived in REYKJAVÍK, capital of Iceland, in the north-west. This rugged island is one of the most active volcanic areas on earth and has many hot springs and mud pools.**

## THE ROUTE

☞ Fly to **BODØ** on the NW coast of Norway. Look down on whales. Take the coastal steamer NE past **TROMSØ** to **NORTH CAPE.**

☞ Continue by steamer to **KIRKENES,** to the SE, near the Russian border. You are in the land of the midnight sun where for parts of the summer the sun never sets and in the winter it seldom rises.

☞ Find your way by husky dog and sledge SW to **KARASJOK**. Do you see those people herding reindeer? They are Sami (Lapps), who have lived here in Europe's last wilderness since ancient times. Continue SW to **KAUTOKEINO.**

☞ Go by bus SE all the way to **ROVANIEMI.** Visit the Santa Claus Workshop Village. Letters are sent here to Santa from children all over the world.

☞ Fly W by ski-plane over the border as far as **ARJEPLOG** in Sweden. You are now beside the deepest of Sweden's many lakes. One of these lakes is said to have a monster!

▱ SEEK THE MAGIC GLOBE
Now it is orange.

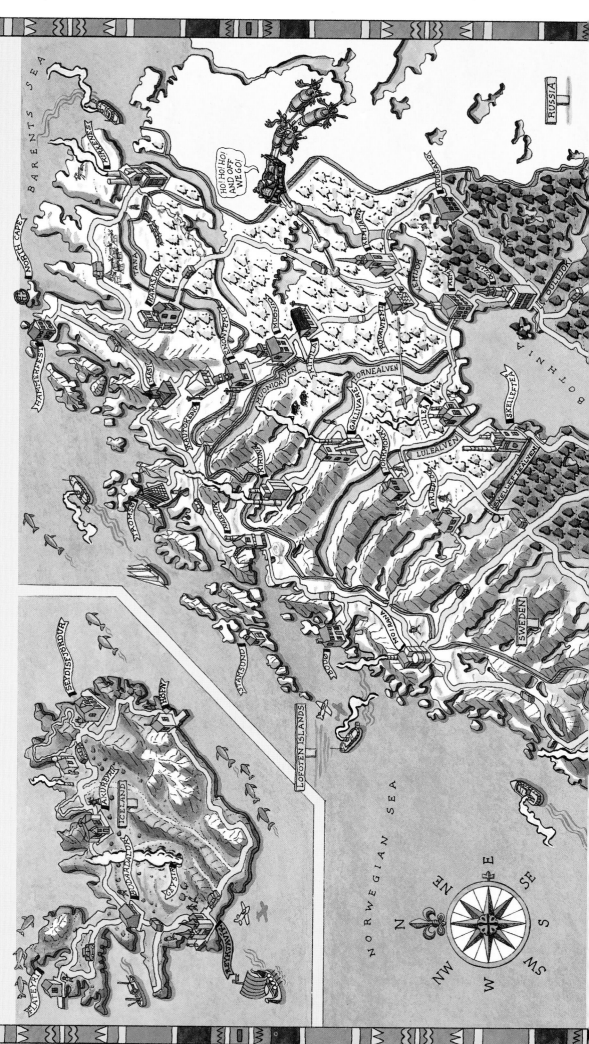

**You have arrived in COPENHAGEN, capital of Denmark, in the south of Scandinavia. Denmark includes over 400 islands.**

☞ THE ROUTE ☜

☞ Are you a Lego fan? Fly W to **BILLUND** and visit Legoland. It's made of over 30 million Lego bricks.

☞ Fly N to **OSLO**, capital of Norway, and visit the Viking Ship Museum.

☞ Take the train W to **BERGEN**. Go by ship along the coast past **ÅLESUND** to **TRONDHEIM**, to the NE. On the way explore the fjords – deep fingers of sea reaching between steep mountains.

☞ Take the bus SE all the way to **FALUN** in Sweden. Look down into the giant copper pit, 99 m deep and 396 m across.

☞ Go SW by road to **ÖREBRO** and visit the medieval castle. Then go E to **STOCKHOLM**, Sweden's capital.

☞ Go NE by ferry to **TURKU**, the oldest town in Finland. Then cycle SE to **HELSINKI**, Finland's capital. You are on the King's Road, the old route that links Norway, Sweden and Finland with St Petersburg in Russia.

☞ Now take a bus NE to **SAVONLINNA**. Go fishing, canoeing and rowing on the lakes. Finland has 198,000 lakes.

☞ **SEEK THE MAGIC GLOBE**
Now it is red and yellow.

**You have arrived in MURMANSK, a major port in north-west Russia, the largest country in the world. It stretches for more than 9,000 km from west to east.**

### ~ THE ROUTE ~

☞ Go S by train to **ST PETERSBURG**. Do you see that statue of a man on horseback? It's Peter the Great, who built this city on marshy swampland and made it Russia's capital.

☞ Go by road SE to **MOSCOW**, now the capital of Russia. Travel around the city by metro and see magnificent underground stations decorated with chandeliers and statues. Then go to the ballet.

☞ Continue by car past **BRYANSK** to **KIEV**, capital of the Ukraine, to the SW. Go to the circus and see the clowns.

☞ Go by road SE to **ODESSA** and cross the water to **YALTA**. You are now in the region known as the Crimea. Visit Fairy-Tale Valley and see statues of characters from well-known fairy stories.

☞ Continue by boat SE across **THE BLACK SEA** to Georgia and tour the capital, **TBILISI**. Go hiking in the mountains called the Caucasus, where many people live to be more than 100 years old.

☞ Follow the road SE to **BAKU**, capital of Azerbaijan. You are now beside the Caspian Sea, the largest lake in the world. Like to try some caviare? It is made from the tiny eggs of large fish – sturgeon – that swim in the lake.

☞ **SEEK THE MAGIC GLOBE**
   Now it is red and blue.

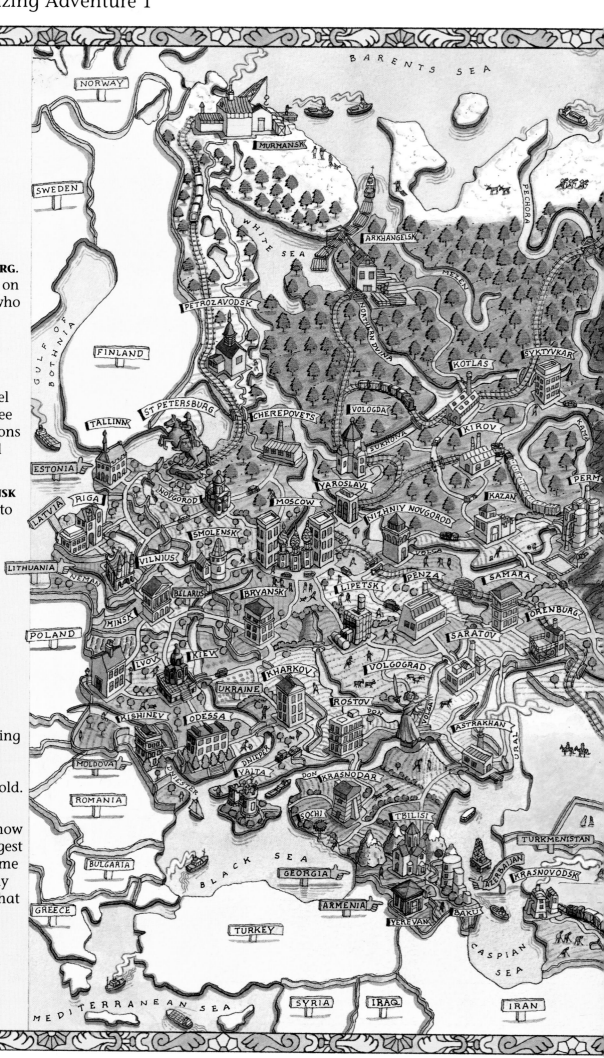

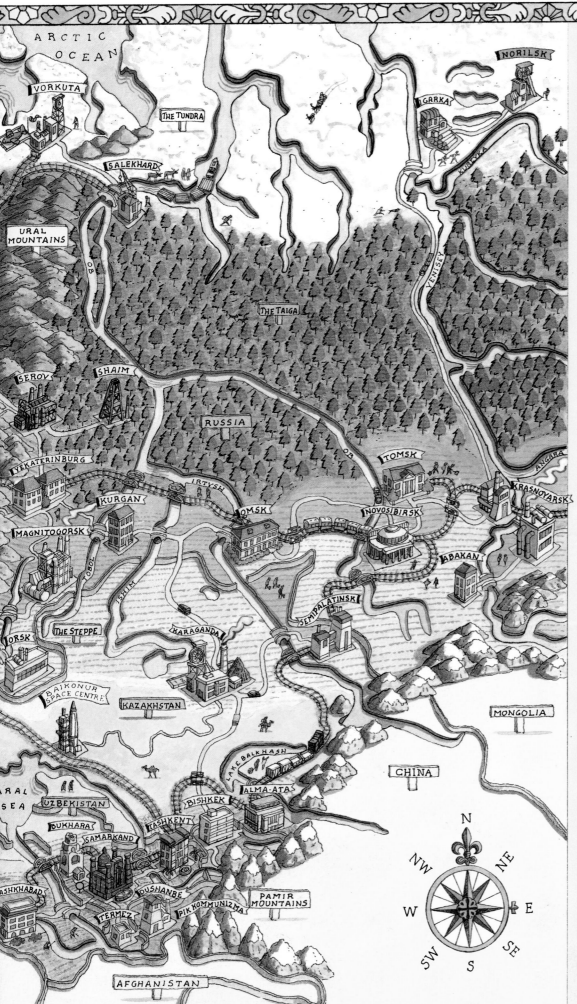

**You have arrived in NORILSK in the north-east. You are in Siberia, the vast eastern region of Russia, which continues for thousands of kilometres to the east from here.**

### ～ THE ROUTE ～

☞ Take the road past **IGARKA** all the way to **KRASNOYARSK,** to the S. You are travelling through the *taiga* – coniferous forest. This forest is the largest in the world. Brown bear, elk and wolves live here.

☞ Go SW to **NOVOSIBIRSK** on the Trans-Siberian railway, the longest railway in the world. Cold and hungry? Try Siberian *pelmeni* – minced meat in parcels of pasta, served with vinegar.

☞ Sail NW along the **RIVER OB** all the way to **SALEKHARD**. Tour the *tundra* – flat, treeless land – where people have lived for centuries raising reindeer.

☞ Take the road NW to **VORKUTA**. Then fly S over the **URAL MOUNTAINS** to **SEROV**. These mountains form the natural frontier between Europe in the W and Asia in the E.

☞ Take the road to **KURGAN**, to the SE. Then go on by bus across the *steppe* – flat grassy plain – to **KARAGANDA** in Kazakhstan.

☞ Interested in space travel? Go to **BAIKONUR SPACE CENTRE**, to the SW. Yuri Gagarin, the first man in space, was launched from here in 1961.

☞ Go by train SE to **TASHKENT**, capital of Uzbekistan. Then travel W to **SAMARKAND**. You are on the ancient Silk Road, once the only link between China and the West.

☞ **SEEK THE MAGIC GLOBE**

Now it is orange.